RADIATION

Design	Cooper-West
Editor	Margaret Fagan
Researcher	Cecilia Weston-Baker
Illustrator	Louise Nevett
Consultant	J. W. Warren Ph.D
	Formerly reader in Physics
	Education, Department of
	Physics, Brunel University, London

Published by Price/Stern/Sloan Publishers, Inc.
360 North La Cienega Boulevard, Los Angeles, California 90048

ISBN: 0-8431-4291-X

THE **HOW AND WHY** WONDER BOOK® OF

RADIATION

MARK PETTIGREW

PRICE/STERN/SLOAN
Publishers, Inc., Los Angeles
1987

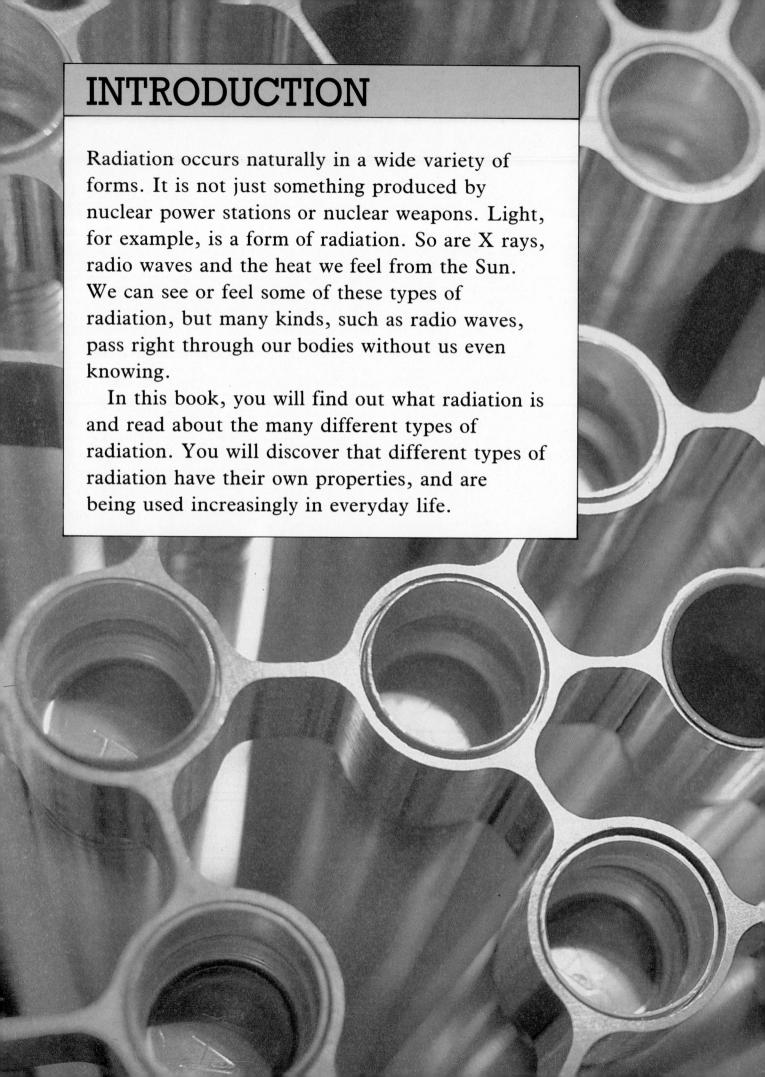

INTRODUCTION

Radiation occurs naturally in a wide variety of forms. It is not just something produced by nuclear power stations or nuclear weapons. Light, for example, is a form of radiation. So are X rays, radio waves and the heat we feel from the Sun. We can see or feel some of these types of radiation, but many kinds, such as radio waves, pass right through our bodies without us even knowing.

In this book, you will find out what radiation is and read about the many different types of radiation. You will discover that different types of radiation have their own properties, and are being used increasingly in everyday life.

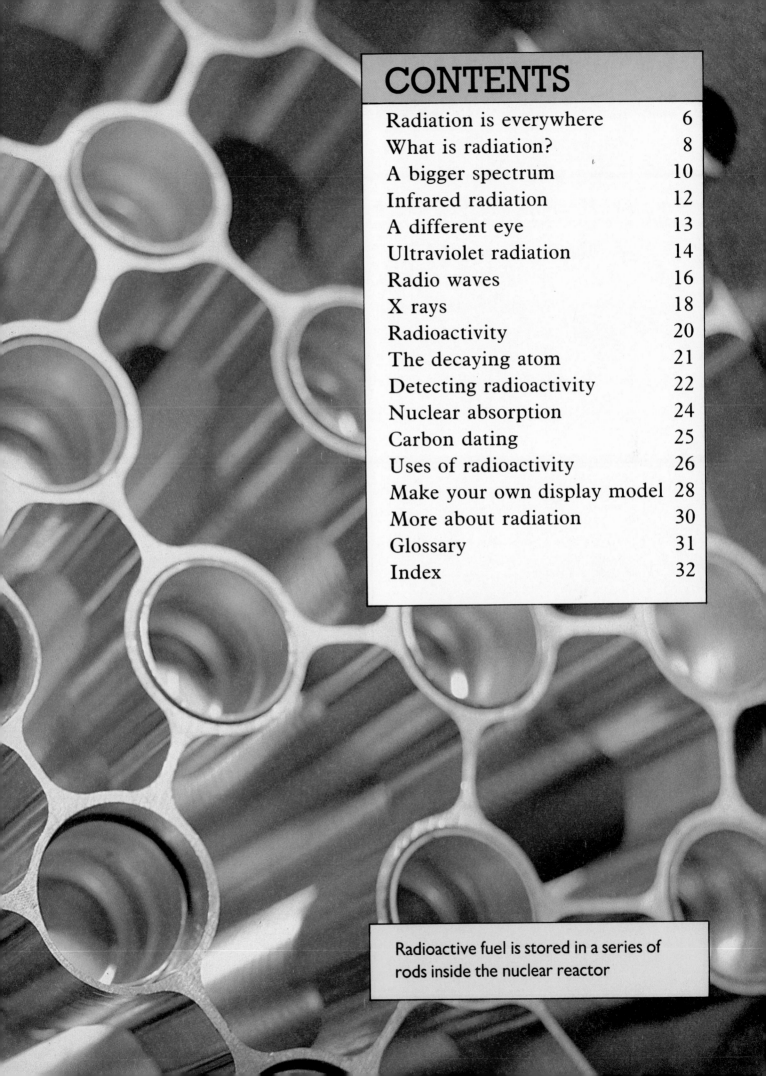

CONTENTS

Radioactive fuel is stored in a series of rods inside the nuclear reactor

RADIATION IS EVERYWHERE

Our bodies are constantly being bombarded by radiation, even though we are usually unaware of it. Most of this radiation reaches us from outer space. For example, the Earth is warmed and lit by radiation from the Sun. The stars and the Sun also produce many different types of invisible radiation. Both visible and invisible radiation have to travel huge distances to reach us. Light radiation from the Sun takes about eight minutes to travel 93 million miles (150 million km) to the Earth. Radiation from the stars travels even further – it can take billions of years for the light from distant stars to reach us!

Radiation also occurs naturally on the Earth's surface. Uranium, for example, is a metal which produces radiation and is used as a fuel in nuclear power stations.

We can see and feel the radiation from the Sun

Radiation also reaches us from the stars

. . . and from uranium which is mined from the Earth

WHAT IS RADIATION?

Radiation is a way of transferring energy from one place – the source – to another place some distance away. Radiation usually travels in straight lines called "rays." On a fine sunny day you can feel the Sun's rays warming your skin. These rays travel through the air without warming it up. But when there are clouds in the sky, they block the Sun's rays and you no longer feel the Sun's warmth.

All radiation can be dangerous, depending on how much energy is transferred from the source of radiation. Some high power lasers can be concentrated to produce a beam of light radiation that will transfer enough energy to cut through sheets of steel. Yet most lasers do not transfer enough to be dangerous. You can quite safely place your hand in front of most lasers.

Heat as radiation

We can see the glow of an electric heater, and we can feel the warmth, yet we cannot see anything traveling through the air to our bodies. Most of the energy sent out by an electric heater is sent out as invisible rays of radiation, and it is the energy transferred by this radiation that we feel as warmth and see as light.

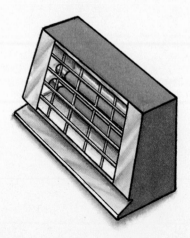

Low power lasers are used to create special lighting effects

A BIGGER SPECTRUM

Light is the only type of radiation that humans can see. The light we can see coming from the Sun is called "white light" but by using a glass prism we can split up white light into a set of colors. We call this the "visible spectrum."

By using different types of instruments, we can discover that visible light is only a small part of a large family of radiation which is called the "electromagnetic spectrum." This includes types of radiation that we cannot see like radio waves, X rays, infrared, ultraviolet and gamma rays. All these types of electromagnetic radiation travel at the same speed – known as the speed of light, 186,000 miles (300,000 km) per second.

The visible spectrum consists of a sequence of colors, from red to violet. The members of the electromagnetic spectrum also form a sequence, from gamma rays to radio waves.

White light split into a spectrum of colors

White light

Glass prism

| GAMMA RAYS | X RAYS | ULTRAVIOLET RADIATION | LIGHT | INFRARED RADIATION | RADIO WAVES |

ELECTROMAGNETIC SPECTRUM

Radio waves take several seconds to reach an astronaut in space

INFRARED RADIATION

Just outside the visible spectrum on the red side is infrared radiation. Some of the energy from the Sun reaches us as infrared radiation. These infrared rays help to keep the Earth's atmosphere at a temperature at which we can live.

Everything, even if very cold, gives off some infrared radiation. Very hot things such as electric heaters and infrared grills produce a lot of infrared radiation. Some creatures, like tropical snakes, can actually detect their prey because they can feel the infrared radiation from warm-blooded animals. Earthquake victims buried alive under rubble can sometimes be found by using a very sensitive infrared camera that detects the infrared radiation produced by their bodies.

An infrared photograph showing heat loss from a polar bear

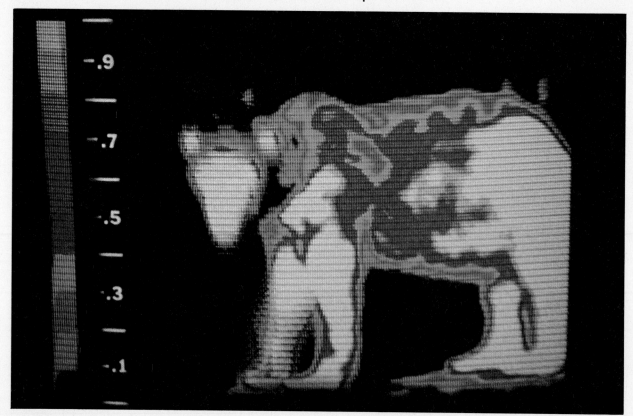

A DIFFERENT EYE

Infrared photographs taken from satellites can show the temperatures of different parts of the landscape. Towns are usually warmer than the surrounding countryside, and rivers and lakes can be a different temperature from the land. The colors in the photograph are not the actual colors of the landscape, but have been chosen to show the differences in temperature. In this photograph, warmer areas show up blue, and colder areas show up red.

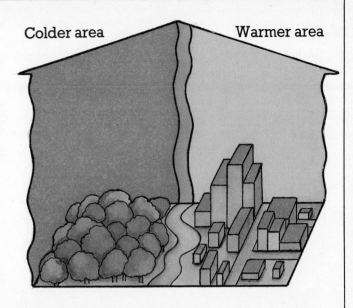

An infrared photograph of London: can you detect the warmer areas?

ULTRAVIOLET RADIATION

Ultraviolet rays are just past the violet end of the visible spectrum. The Sun produces some ultraviolet radiation, and this is what causes a suntan or sunburn.

Ultraviolet rays are invisible to our eyes, but they can be detected when they hit something "fluorescent." Fluorescent substances react to ultraviolet radiaton by producing visible light that we see as a glow. By using mixtures of fluorescent substances, different colors of light are produced. Detergent manufacturers often add a fluorescent substance to washing powders. This makes white clothes appear brighter by producing extra white light when ultraviolet rays from the Sun fall on them.

Light and infrared rays from the Sun can pass through glass. This allows plants in a greenhouse to grow. Ultraviolet rays are stopped by glass. So people who work in greenhouses feel the Sun's heat all day but do not become sun-tanned. People who lie outside in the Sun, however, do become tanned.

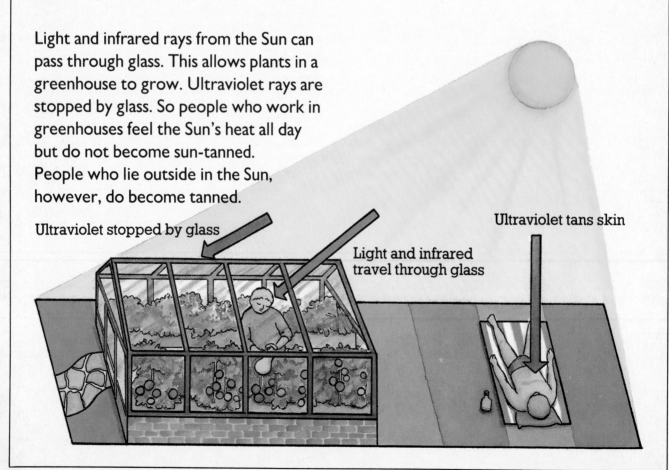

Ultraviolet stopped by glass

Light and infrared travel through glass

Ultraviolet tans skin

Fluorescent lights are used in brightly colored advertising displays

RADIO WAVES

Radio and television signals usually reach our homes as radio waves, another type of electromagnetic radiation. However, unlike light, radio waves can pass through walls and buildings. Radio waves spread out from a transmitting aerial in all directions, just like the small waves that appear when you drop a stone into a pond.

Microwaves are closely related to radio waves. They are used in radar, for example. Unlike radio waves, their energy can be concentrated in a thin beam. This beam of microwave radiation can be used to determine the position of a far away object, like a plane. As the beam of microwave radiation bounces off the plane, the time it takes to return to the aerial is measured by a computer. The computer can then calculate the plane's exact location.

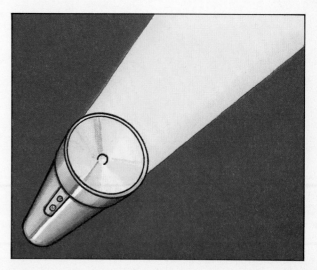

Most types of radiation will usually spread out in all directions, like the light from a bulb. By placing a curved reflector behind a flashlight bulb, the radiation can be concentrated into a narrow beam. A beam of microwaves is produced in a similar way by the curved reflector of a radar transmitter.

Radar signals sent from a transmitter are monitored in the air-traffic control room

X RAYS

X rays are a high-energy type of electromagnetic radiation. Although they are produced naturally by the Sun, the X rays we use are artificially created. X rays can pass through many of the substances that stop light. For example, they can pass through skin and cloth, but are absorbed by substances like bone and metal. X-ray cameras are used in hospitals to examine broken bones, and in airports to check for hidden weapons.

Large quantities of X rays can damage the cells in our bodies. However, it is quite safe to have an X-ray photograph taken occasionally. But the people who take these photographs hundreds of times a week stand behind a screen to avoid the harmful effects of radiation.

An X-ray camera produces X rays, which are directed toward a piece of photographic film. The more X rays that hit the film in one place, the darker the film becomes at that place. The object to be examined is placed between the source of X rays and the film. X rays are absorbed by bone, and so very little radiation passes through the bone to the film behind, which remains white or pale gray. X rays pass easily through skin and flesh, with only a little being absorbed, and the film behind turns dark gray or black. This produces a kind of "shadow" picture of the bone on the film.

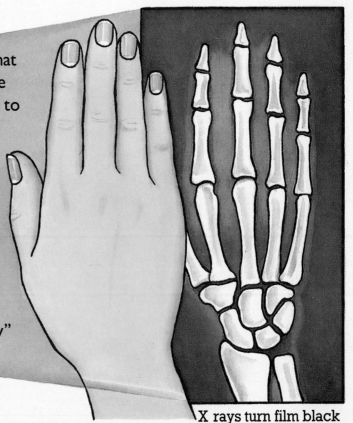

X rays turn film black

18

X rays are used in security checks at airports

RADIOACTIVITY

Everything is made up of millions of atoms. An atom itself is made up of a tiny nucleus, surrounded by electrons. In most substances these atoms remain unchanged because their nuclei are stable. But some substances have unstable nuclei which give off bursts of radiation at any moment. These substances are "radioactive" and the energy they produce is called "nuclear radiation." Radioactive substances produce radiation every time their nuclei change. Eventually, after one or more bursts of nuclear radiation, the nucleus will become stable and therefore non-radioactive.

Radioactive fuel, often uranium, is used in nuclear power stations. The radioactive fuel is placed in a series of fuel rods in the nuclear reactor. As the fuel is used, it produces a great deal of radiation. Thick layers of lead and concrete surround the reactor to protect the environment from this radiation.

Radioactive waste is transported in containers specially designed for safety

THE DECAYING ATOM

The nucleus of an atom is made up of two types of particles: protons and neutrons. Protons carry a positive electric charge, while neutrons carry no charge. The electrons that circle around the nucleus each carry a negative charge. The charges of the electrons exactly balance the protons. But in the atoms of a radioactive substance, the nucleus carries too many or too few neutrons and this makes it unstable. In order to get rid of this instability, bursts of radiation from the nucleus are produced. This radiation is sent out as alpha rays, beta rays or gamma rays. Although all three types of rays can be produced by a radioactive nucleus, they are never all produced by one nucleus at the same time. It is this process of change which is called radioactive decay.

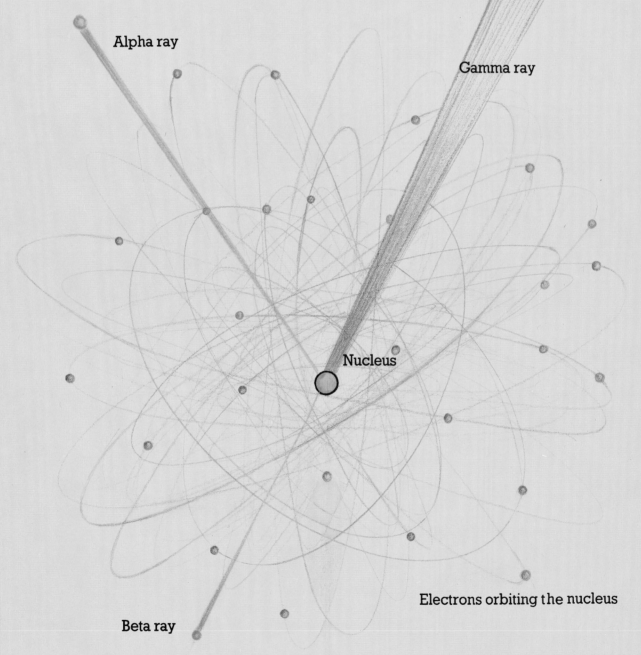

Alpha ray

Gamma ray

Nucleus

Beta ray

Electrons orbiting the nucleus

DETECTING RADIOACTIVITY

Scientists measure the amount of radioactivity in a substance by counting the number of atoms that decay by producing a burst of nuclear radiation. To do this, they use a Geiger counter, a sensitive instrument which can detect small amounts of radioactivity due to radiation from alpha, beta and gamma rays.

However, no matter how much radioactivity a substance has to start with, we find that *half* this radioactivity is lost after a certain amount of time. We call this period of time a "half-life." The half-life of different radioactive substances ranges from less than a second for extremely unstable substances to several billion years. For example, a type of radioactive granite which occurs naturally has a half-life of more than a billion years.

Half-life

Imagine deciding to drink half of what is in a glass of water every day. After one day there would be half a glass of water left. The next day you drink half of this leaving only a quarter, and after three days there would be an eighth left. In this example, the half-life of the water in the glass is one day: the time taken to halve the contents of the glass.

After one day   After two days   After three days

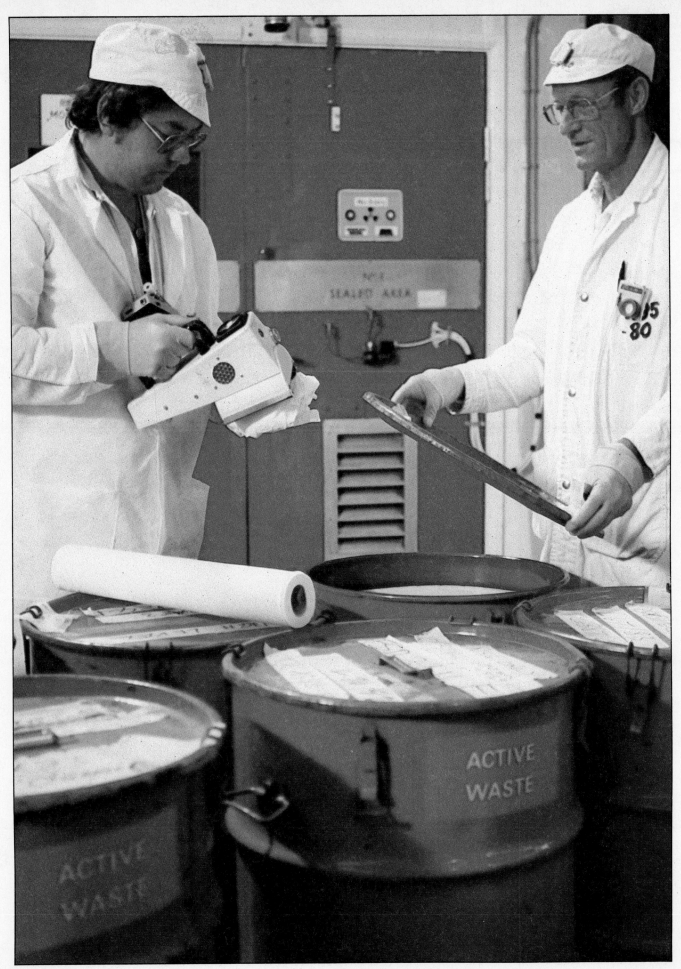

A Geiger counter is used to measure the radiation level from waste materials

NUCLEAR ABSORPTION

Alpha, beta and gamma rays are all very energetic types of nuclear radiation. They even have enough energy to remove the outer electrons from the atoms of the substance through which they pass. When this happens some atoms are left with a positive charge. These atoms are called "ions."

Most things that alpha, beta and gamma rays can do depend on their ability to "ionize" a substance. This is their way of transferring energy from one place to another. And as alpha, beta and gamma rays pass on their energy to a substance, they themselves are *absorbed*. Alpha and beta rays are more easily absorbed than gamma. Gamma rays can penetrate thick steel or lead before they are finally absorbed by concrete.

Beta rays can be used to measure the thickness of a thin sheet of metal. As the metal is produced it passes between a source of beta rays and a detector. The amount of beta radiation which passes through the metal is very accurately measured by a Geiger counter. The thicker metal absorbs more beta radiation. This information is used to control the thickness of the metal.

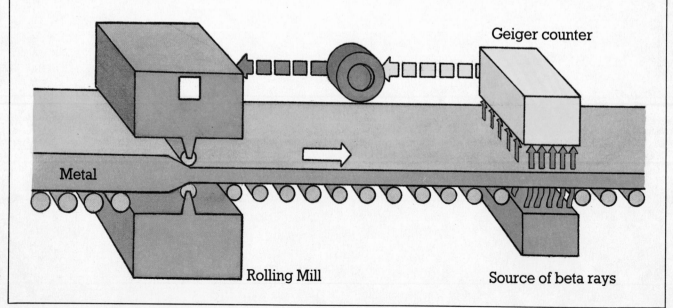

Geiger counter

Metal

Rolling Mill

Source of beta rays

CARBON DATING

The carbon dioxide in the air contains a small amount of radioactive carbon. All living things contain a little of this radioactive carbon. Radioactive carbon has a half-life of about 5,500 years. After this time, half the amount of radioactive carbon will have disappeared. Trees and plants take up the carbon dioxide from the air, and animals eat the plants. When a plant, tree or animal dies, it stops taking in any more radioactive carbon. By measuring the amount of radioactive carbon at any time after death, the age of the plant, tree or animal can be calculated.

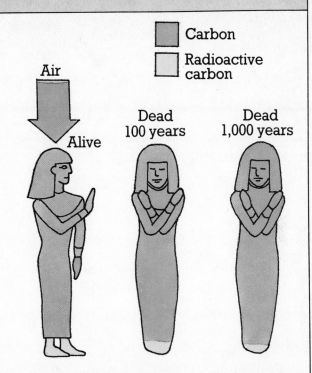

Carbon dating shows that this Egyptian mummy is over 2,000 years old

USES OF RADIOACTIVITY

The fact that radiation can kill living cells is also used to our advantage. For example, gamma rays are used to kill the bacteria and viruses which cause disease. This is called "sterilization." Medical equipment is often sterilized using gamma radiation. Food could be sterilized in the same way to keep it fresh for a very long time. Gamma rays can be used in the treatment of cancer by killing the dangerous cells in the body. Small amounts of radioactive substances called "tracers" can be put into a person's body. These tracers are then followed as they travel through the body by detecting the radiation they produce. In this way, it is possible to find out if the person's body is working normally.

Syringes are sterilized by gamma rays before they are used

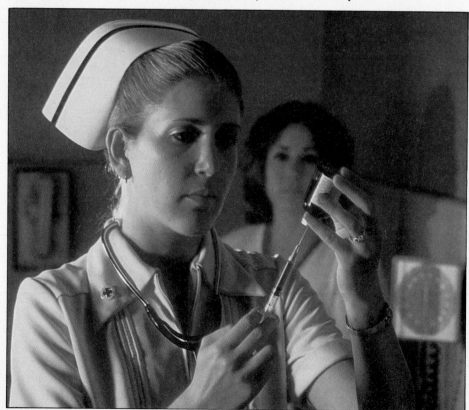

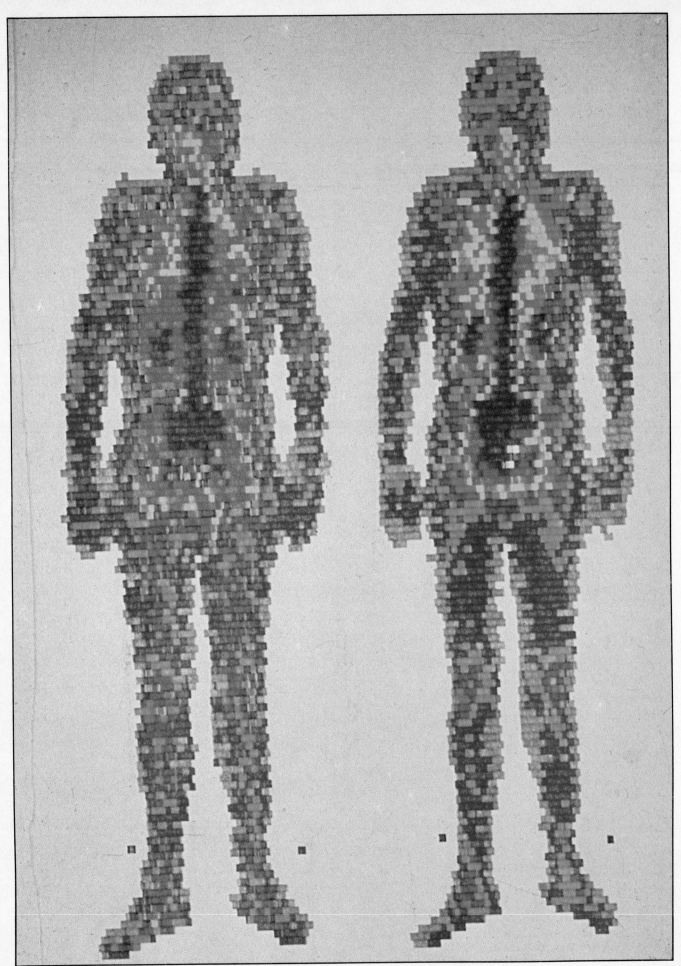

A front and back body scan of a healthy person using a radioactive tracer

MAKE YOUR OWN DISPLAY MODEL

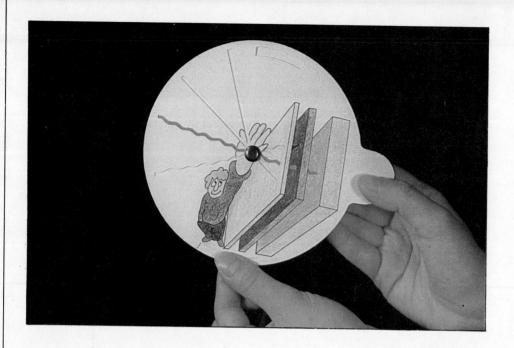

Different types of radiation can pass through substances more or less easily. For example, radio waves can pass through buildings but are stopped by water. Light rays from the Sun pass through great depths of water until they are absorbed; thus the ocean floor is often completely dark.

By following these instructions and diagrams, you can make your own display model which shows how some types of radiation are absorbed. For example, by turning the disk you can see that X rays pass through your hand and through a sheet of aluminum but are absorbed by lead. Can you see which type of ray is the most penetrating?

Making the model

Trace the drawings on the opposite page. Then transfer one tracing onto a piece of cardboard. Label each piece of cardboard as shown and color in. Cut out the cardboard and also the shaded areas on disk A. Hold the pieces of cardboard together with a thumbtack. When you turn the lower disk B, the colored ray will appear through the cutout slits on disk A and match with the different names as they appear through the window.

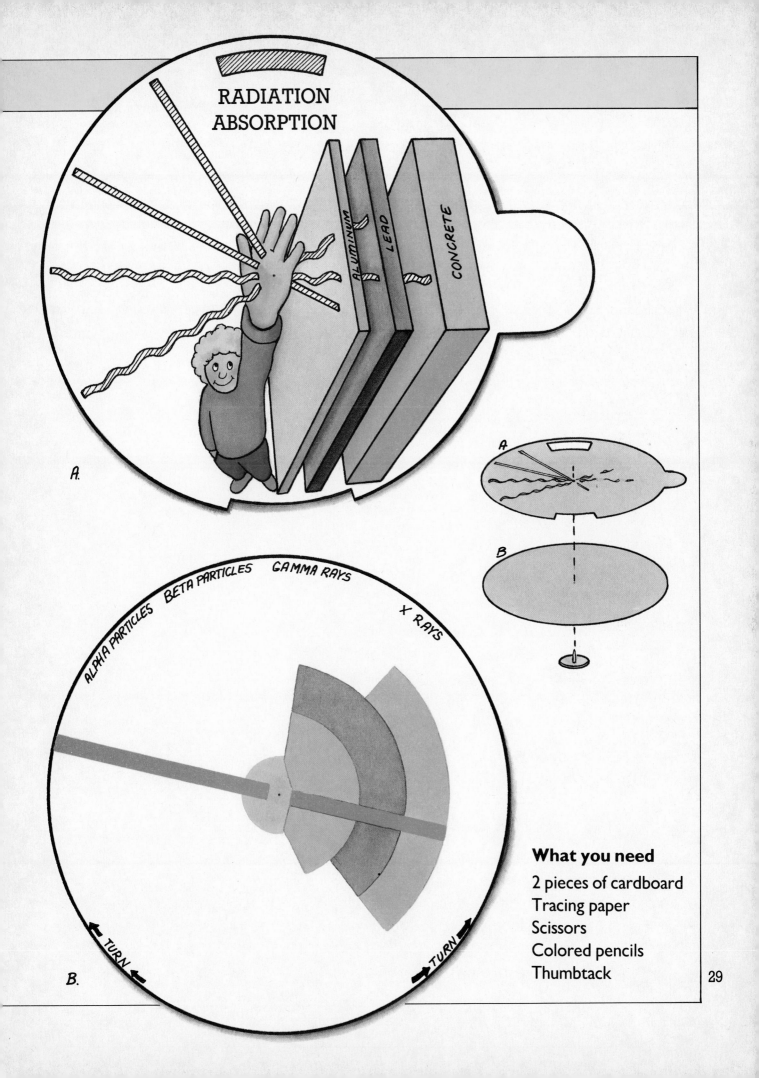

RADIATION
ABSORPTION

A.

ALUMINUM
LEAD
CONCRETE

B.

ALPHA PARTICLES   BETA PARTICLES   GAMMA RAYS   X RAYS

TURN   TURN

A

B

What you need

2 pieces of cardboard
Tracing paper
Scissors
Colored pencils
Thumbtack

29

MORE ABOUT RADIATION

Nuclear radiation and X rays in high doses are dangerous to all living things. However, our bodies are exposed to various sources of relatively harmless quantities of both these types of radiation. Most of this comes from natural sources. This diagram shows approximately how much of this radiation comes from different places in an industrial society.

There are radioactive substances present in the air we breathe, in our food and drink, in the ground and in our buildings. We also receive nuclear radiation from outer space. Most X rays are from man-made sources, and are used in medicine. Only a small amount of nuclear radiation is due to nuclear power stations and nuclear weapons.

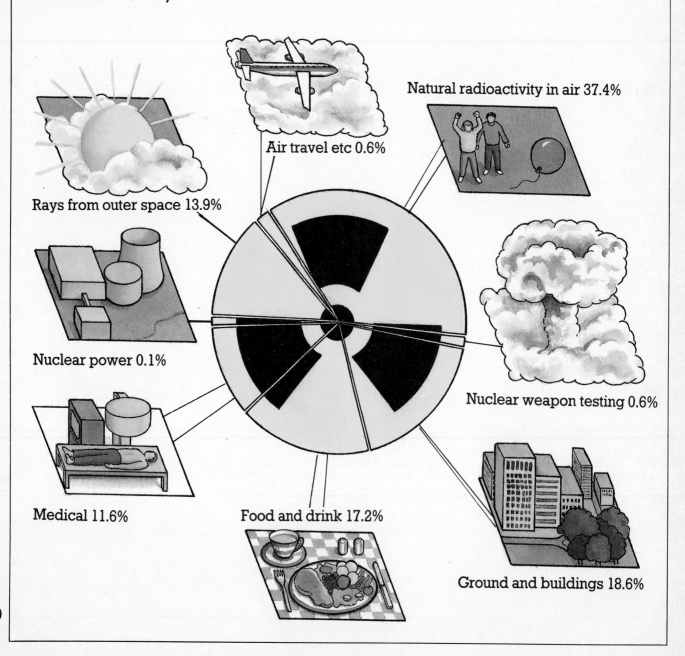

Air travel etc 0.6%

Natural radioactivity in air 37.4%

Rays from outer space 13.9%

Nuclear power 0.1%

Nuclear weapon testing 0.6%

Medical 11.6%

Food and drink 17.2%

Ground and buildings 18.6%

GLOSSARY

Absorption
As radiation passes through a substance, it gradually loses energy and is absorbed.

Decay
When the nucleus of a radioactive atom produces a single burst of nuclear radiation it is changed into the nucleus of a different atom. This is known as radioactive decay.

Electromagnetic spectrum
A large family of radiation which includes light, infrared, ultraviolet, X rays, radio waves and gamma rays.

Electron
An electron orbits around the atom's nucleus. Every electron carries a negative electric charge.

Half-life
The time taken for half the energy of a radioactive substance to be discharged by bursts of nuclear radiation.

Ion
Usually an atom has neither a positive nor a negative charge. But when an atom loses or gains an electron, it becomes positively or negatively charged and is known as an ion.

Neutron
In the nucleus of the atom are particles, called neutrons. These never carry an electric charge.

Nuclear radiation
The nucleus of a radioactive atom gives out energy in the form of alpha, beta and gamma rays. Because this radiation comes from the nucleus, it is called nuclear radiation.

Proton
These particles carry a positive electric charge in the nucleus.

Radioactive
Substances which are radioactive have their own energy because of their unstable nuclei. In the nucleus of a radioactive atom there are either too many or too few neutrons.

Ray
A way of transferring energy from one place to another without changing the substance through which it passes. For example, rays of heat travel to Earth without warming the air above.

Stable
A stable substance is one which is not radioactive because it has a balance of neutrons and protons in its nucleus.

INDEX

Photographic Credits:
Cover and pages 6 and 26, Art Directors; title page and page 12, Spectrum; contents page, Paul Brierly; pages 7 and 23, UKAEA; page 7, Tony Stone Associates; pages 9 and 25, Zefa; page 11, ESA; pages 13, 17 (inset), 20 and 27, Science Photo Library; page 15, Robert Harding; page 17, Flight/QPL; page 19 (both), IAL; page 28, Cooper–West.

PRINTED IN BELGIUM BY

proost
INTERNATIONAL BOOK PRODUCTION